Christelle Huet-Gomez
Photography by Valéry Guédes

MAGIC CAKES

Three cakes in one:
one mixture, one bake, three delicious layers

hardie grant books

Contents

What is a magic cake?

What does a cake contain to deserve the name magic?

Magic cakes are made simply of eggs, sugar, flour, butter and milk. So what's magic about that, you might ask. There may be nothing unusual about the ingredients, but the magic happens in the baking. The batter of the cake is very liquid, so it divides into three layers by itself, each with its own texture and flavour:

– the base of the cake is a dense, moist cake base;

– a light delicate cream forms in the middle;

– the top layer is a lovely light Genoise sponge.

How is this even possible?

The egg yolks, beaten with the sugar, butter, flour and milk, form the first two layers of the magic cake: the base and the cream. What happens is that slow cooking at 150°C (300°F/Gas 2) allows the bottom of the cake to cook like a cake without cooking the upper part, which retains its creamy texture. For this reason it is best to use a conventional oven rather than a fan-assisted one. The beaten egg whites form the Genoise sponge layer. They do not blend with the milk and instead remain floating on top of the cake!

cream

Genoise
sponge

dense, moist
cake base

The five golden rules

One mixture, one bake and the result: three cakes in one. Just follow the rules below and this easy-to-make dessert will cause a sensation!

1. The tin size

It is important that the size of your baking tin corresponds exactly to the quantity of ingredients in the recipe. If your tin is too small, you might not be able to pour all your beaten egg whites on top, resulting in a Genoise layer that is too thin. Conversely, if your tin is too big, each layer will be too thin and it will be difficult to tell them apart. For the majority of the recipes in this book, we use a 24 cm (9½ in) round cake tin.

2. The egg whites

To incorporate the egg whites into the liquid mixture, it is best to use a whisk and work the mass gently so that it doesn't dissolve into the batter: large lumps should remain. In fact it is difficult to incorporate egg whites into a liquid mixture using a wooden spoon. The whites floating on the surface of the tin will be smoothed with the blade of a knife before the cake is put in the oven.

3. Baking

If the cake is not fully baked, it will not hold together. If it is overcooked, the layer of cream will disappear. At the end of the baking time given in the recipe, the cake should still have a slight wobble, which will set when it is chilled. The upper layer – the Genoise sponge – should be well baked and golden. All the cooking times indicated in the recipes correspond to a conventional oven. If your oven is fan-assisted, you can reduce all the temperatures by 10°C (50°F).

4. Turning out the cake

It is vital to wait for the magic cake to set before turning it out. It should be kept chilled for at least 2 hours. It will be easier to turn out if you use a silicone cake tin. Otherwise, it is best to line your tin with baking parchment.

5. Tasting

The magic cake will taste better after spending a few hours, or even overnight, in the fridge, giving the flavours time to develop. So don't leave it until the last minute to make and be patient!

The important stages in preparing the batter

– Beat the egg yolks and sugar together well, until the mixture whitens.
– Incorporate the egg whites gently using the whisk, without mixing too much. You should still have large lumps.

Magic Vanilla Cake

Serves 8
Preparation: 20 minutes
Cooking time: 50 minutes
Resting time: 1 + 2 hours

2 vanilla pods
500 ml (17 fl oz) milk
4 eggs, separated
150 g (5 oz) caster (superfine
  sugar
1 sachet vanilla sugar
1 tablespoon water
125 g (4 oz) butter
110 g (3¾ oz) plain (all-purpose)
  flour
pinch of salt

24 cm (9½ in) cake tin, silicone or
greased with butter and lined with
baking parchment

Split the vanilla pods down the middle and scrape out the seeds with the blade of a knife. Heat the milk with the vanilla seeds and the open pods. Bring to the boil, then immediately remove from the heat and leave to infuse for at least 1 hour. The more infused the vanilla, the more intense the taste.

Preheat the oven to 150°C (300°F/Gas 2).

Whisk the yolks with the sugar and water until the mixture whitens. Melt the butter and stir it into the mixture. Fold in the flour and salt and beat for a few minutes until well combined.

Remove the vanilla pods from the milk. Pour it into the batter little by little, whisking constantly.

Beat the egg whites until stiff and, using a whisk, gently incorporate them into the batter. Pour the batter into the greased tin, smooth the surface with the blade of a knife and bake in the oven for 50 minutes. When the cake comes out of the oven it will wobble slightly.

Before turning it out, leave it to set in the fridge for at least 2 hours. Serve chilled.

Chef's tip

Dust the cake with icing (confectioners') sugar.

White Chocolate Cake

Serves 10
Preparation: 20 minutes
Cooking time: 50 minutes
Resting time: 2 hours

3 eggs, separated
75 g (2½ oz) caster (superfine)
   sugar
1 tablespoon water
1 teaspoon vanilla extract
75 g (2½ oz) butter
120 g (4 oz) white chocolate
75 g (2½ oz) plain (all-purpose)
   flour
pinch of salt
370 ml (12½ fl oz) milk, at room
   temperature

10 cm (4 in) x 24 cm (9½ in)
deep, square cake tin, silicone or
greased with butter and lined with
baking parchment

Preheat the oven to 150°C (300°F / Gas 2).

Whisk the egg yolks with the sugar and water until the mixture whitens. Add the vanilla extract.

Melt the butter and white chocolate together. Gently stir into the egg mixture. Then add the flour and salt. Beat for a few minutes. Pour in the milk little by little, whisking constantly.

Beat the egg whites until stiff and, using a whisk, gently incorporate them into the batter.

Pour the batter into the greased cake tin, smooth the surface with the blade of a knife and bake in the oven for 50 minutes. When the cake comes out of the oven it will wobble slightly.

Before turning it out, leave it to set in the fridge for at least 2 hours. Serve chilled.

Chef's tip

To add a ganache topping, melt 150 g (5 oz) white chocolate then, away from the heat, add 70 ml (2¼ fl oz) double (full-fat) cream or whipping cream. Chill in the fridge for at least 2 hours, then whip the ganache for about 10 minutes until thick. Dust with icing (confectioners') sugar before serving.

Salted Butter Caramel Cake

Serves 8
Preparation: 45 minutes
Cooking time: 5 + 55 minutes
Resting time: 2 hours

Caramel
300 g (10½ oz) caster (superfine)
  sugar
a few drops of lemon juice
150 ml (5 fl oz) single cream,
  warmed
75 g (2½ oz) salted butter, cold

Cake
450 ml (15 fl oz) milk
4 eggs, separated
70 g (2½ oz) salted butter, melted
90 g (3¼ oz) plain (all-purpose)
  flour
pinch of salt

24 cm (9½ in) cake tin, silicone or
greased with butter and lined with
baking parchment

Begin by preparing the caramel. Heat the sugar and lemon juice in
a large thick-bottomed saucepan until the sugar melts and turns a
caramel colour. It is best to check the colour with a wooden spoon
as the caramel can look dark in the bottom of the saucepan. Add the
warm cream, taking care not to splash. Remove the saucepan from the
heat and stir in the salted butter.

Set aside 100 g (3½ oz) caramel and pour the milk into the remaining
caramel. Bring to the boil until the caramel is fully dissolved in the
milk. Leave to cool.

Preheat the oven to 150°C (300°F/Gas 2).

Beat the yolks with the melted butter. Fold in the flour and salt then
pour in the caramel milk little by little, beating constantly.

Beat the egg whites until stiff and, using a whisk, gently incorporate
them into the batter. Pour the batter into the greased cake tin, smooth
the surface with the blade of a knife and bake in the oven for 55 minutes.
When the cake comes out of the oven it will wobble slightly.

Before turning it out, leave it to set in the fridge for at least 2 hours.
Serve chilled.

Chef's tip

Serve the cake with the remaining caramel sauce and a scattering of
pine nuts.

Coffee Cake

Serves 8
Preparation: 25 minutes
Cooking time: 5 + 45 minutes
Resting time: 2 hours

500 ml (17 fl oz) milk
30 g (1 oz) instant coffee
4 eggs, separated
150 g (5 oz) caster (superfine)
  sugar
1 tablespoon water
125 g (4 oz) butter
115 g (4 oz) plain (all-purpose)
  flour
pinch of salt

20 cm (8 in) rectangle cake tin,
silicone or greased with butter and
lined with baking parchment

Preheat the oven to 150°C (300°F/Gas 2).

Heat the milk and coffee in a saucepan until the coffee is fully dissolved. Allow to cool. Beat the egg yolks with the sugar and water until the mixture whitens. Melt the butter and pour it into the mixture. Then fold in the flour and salt. Pour in the milky coffee little by little, beating constantly.

Beat the egg whites until stiff and, using a whisk, gently incorporate them into the batter. Pour the batter into the greased cake tin, smooth the surface with the blade of a knife and bake in the oven for 45 minutes. When the cake comes out of the oven it will wobble slightly.

Before turning it out, leave it to set in the fridge for at least 2 hours. Serve chilled.

Chef's tip

Make a chocolate icing by melting 100 g (3½ oz) dark chocolate in 50 ml (2 fl oz) single cream and drizzle it all over the cake.

Praline Cake

Preparation: 20 minutes
Cooking time: 50 minutes
Resting time: 2 hours

4 eggs, separated
100 g (3½ oz) caster (superfine)
  sugar
1 tablespoon water
100 g (3½ oz) praline paste
80 g (3 oz) butter, melted
80 g (3 oz) plain (all-purpose)
  flour
pinch of salt
450 ml (15 fl oz) milk, at room
  temperature

24 cm (9½ in) cake tin, silicone or
greased with butter and lined with
baking parchment

Preheat the oven to 150°C (300°F/Gas 2).

Beat the egg yolks with the sugar and water until the mixture whitens.
Add the praline paste, then the melted butter. Fold in the flour and
salt. Beat for a few minutes more. Pour in the milk little by little,
beating constantly.

Beat the egg whites until stiff and, using a whisk, gently incorporate
them into the batter. Pour the batter into the greased cake tin, smooth
the surface with the blade of a knife and bake in the oven for
50 minutes. When the cake comes out of the oven it will wobble
slightly. Before turning it out, leave it to set in the fridge for at least
2 hours.

Chef's tip

Sprinkle the cake with crushed praline nuts.

You can also decorate with caramelised whole hazelnuts.

Chocolate and Hazelnut Cake

Serves 8
Preparation: 20 minutes
Cooking time: 50 minutes
Resting time: 2 hours

4 eggs, separated
100 g (3½ oz) caster (superfine)
    sugar
1 tablespoon water
100 g (3½ oz) chocolate hazelnut
    spread
80 g (3 oz) butter
90 g (3¼ oz) plain (all-purpose)
    flour
pinch of salt
450 ml (15 fl oz) milk, at room
    temperature

20 cm (8 in) square cake tin,
silicone or greased with butter and
lined with baking parchment

Preheat the oven to 150°C (300°F/Gas 2).

Whisk the egg yolks with the sugar and water until the mixture whitens. Stir in the spread. Melt the butter and pour it into the mixture. Then fold in the flour and salt. Beat for a few minutes more. Pour in the milk little by little, beating constantly.

Beat the egg whites until stiff and, using a whisk, gently incorporate them into the batter. Pour the batter into the greased cake tin, smooth the surface with the blade of a knife and bake in the oven for 50 minutes. When the cake comes out of the oven it will wobble slightly. Before turning it out, leave it to set in the fridge for at least 2 hours.

Chef's tip

Decorate with a few crushed hazelnuts.

You can also make a chocolate icing by mixing 175 g (6 oz) chocolate hazelnut spread with 250 ml (8½ fl oz) whipping cream. Chill in the fridge for 2 hours then whip until it thickens.

Lemon and Poppy Seed Cake

Serves 8
Preparation: 30 minutes
Cooking time: 50 minutes
Resting time: 2 hours

4 eggs, separated
150 g (5 oz) caster (superfine)
   sugar
125 g (4 oz) butter
125 g (4 oz) plain (all-purpose)
   flour
30 g (1 oz) poppy seeds
pinch of salt
400 ml (13 fl oz) milk, at room
   temperature
juice and zest of 2 lemons

24 cm (9½ in) cake tin, silicone or
greased with butter and lined with
baking parchment

Preheat the oven to 150°C (300°F/Gas 2).

Beat the egg yolks with the sugar until the mixture whitens. Melt the butter and pour it into the mixture. Then add the flour, poppy seeds and salt. Beat for a few minutes, then pour in the milk little by little, whisking constantly. Add the lemon zest and 100 ml (3½ fl oz) juice into the batter.

Beat the egg whites until stiff and, using a whisk, gently incorporate them into the batter. Pour the batter into the greased cake tin, smooth the surface with the blade of a knife and bake in the oven for 50 minutes. When the cake comes out of the oven it will wobble slightly. Before turning it out, leave it to set in the fridge for at least 2 hours. Serve chilled.

Chef's tip

If you like, decorate with a few lemon quarters, fresh mint and sprinkle with poppy seeds.

You can also make an icing by whipping 300 ml (10 fl oz) chilled whipping cream with 150 g (5 oz) mascarpone until thick.
Then gradually pour in 45 g (1¾ oz) caster (superfine) sugar, whipping constantly.

Rose and Blueberry Cupcakes

Serves 8
Preparation: 35 minutes
Cooking time: 27 minutes
Resting time: 2 + 1 hour

Icing
50 g (2 oz) white chocolate
100 ml (3½ fl oz) whipping cream
10 g (½ oz) caster (superfine) sugar

Base
2 eggs, separated
60 g (2 oz) caster (superfine) sugar
1 tablespoon rose water
60 g (2 oz) butter
55 g (2 oz) plain (all-purpose) flour
pinch of salt
250 ml (8½ fl oz) milk, at room
   temperature
100 g (3½ oz) blueberries

Silicone muffin cases, greased with
butter

Melt the white chocolate in the microwave or in a bain-marie. At the same time, heat half of the cream in a saucepan. Pour this cream, a third at a time, onto the melted chocolate, mixing well after each pouring. Then incorporate the rest of the cream. Chill in the fridge for at least 2 hours.

Preheat the oven to 150°C (300°F/Gas 2).

Beat the egg yolks with the sugar and rose water until the mixture whitens. Melt the butter and stir it into the mixture. Fold in the flour and salt, then beat for a few more minutes. Pour in the milk little by little, whisking constantly.

Beat the egg whites until stiff and, using a whisk, gently incorporate them into the batter. Sprinkle blueberries inside the muffin tins. These will move into the middle of the cakes by themselves as they bake. Pour the batter on top and bake in the oven for 27 minutes. Before turning the cakes out, leave to set in the fridge for at least 1 hour.

Take the icing out of the fridge and whip for about 10 minutes, incorporating the sugar little by little. Decorate the cupcakes with the whipped icing to serve.

Chef's tip

Make the icing first as it should rest in the fridge for a few hours.

Add a few blueberries on top of the whipped icing to finish.

Caramelised Apple Cake

Serves 8
Preparation: 30 minutes
Cooking time: 10 + 55 minutes
Resting time: 2 hours

Caramelised apple
3 apples, peeled, cored and diced
30 g (1 oz) caster (supefine) sugar
20 g (¾ oz) salted butter

Cake
4 eggs, separated
120 g (4 oz) caster (superfine) sugar
125 g (4 oz) butter
1 teaspoon vanilla extract
115 g (4 oz) plain (all-purpose)
   flour
pinch of salt
500 ml (17 fl oz) milk, at room
   temperature

24 cm (9½ in) cake tin, silicone or
greased with butter and lined with
baking parchment

Place the apples in a frying pan with the sugar and cook until the apples caramelise, then add the salted butter. Stir and set aside.

Preheat the oven to 150°C (300°F/Gas 2).

Beat the egg yolks with the sugar until the mixture whitens. Melt the butter and pour it into the mixture along with the vanilla extract.

Fold in the flour and salt. Beat for a few minutes, then pour in the milk little by little, whisking constantly.

Beat the egg whites until stiff and, using a whisk, gently incorporate them into the batter.

Arrange the apple slices in the bottom of the greased cake tin, then pour the batter on top. Smooth the surface with the blade of a knife and bake in the oven for 55 minutes.

When the cake comes out of the oven it will wobble slightly. Before turning it out, leave it to set in the fridge for at least 2 hours.

Chef's tip

Decorate the cake with very thin slices of apple or dried apple and a caramel coulis (see page 12).

Pineapple and Coconut Cake

Serves 8
Preparation: 30 minutes
Cooking time: 55 minutes
Resting time: 2 hours

4 eggs, separated
125 g (4 oz) brown sugar
1 sachet vanilla sugar
125 g (4 oz) butter, melted
80 g (3 oz) plain (all-purpose) flour
80 g (3 oz) grated coconut
pinch of salt
200 ml (7 fl oz) milk, at room temperature
250 ml (8½ fl oz) coconut milk
340 g (12 oz) pineapples in syrup

24 cm (9½ in) cake tin, silicone or greased with butter and lined with baking parchment

Preheat the oven to 150°C (300°F/Gas 2).

Beat the egg yolks with the sugar until the mixture whitens. Pour in the melted butter, then add the flour, grated coconut and salt. Beat for a few minutes more. Pour in the milk and coconut milk little by little, beating constantly. The batter should be nice and smooth.

Beat the egg whites until stiff and, using a whisk, gently incorporate them into the batter. Cut the pineapple into small pieces and spread them around the bottom of the greased cake tin. Pour the batter on top, then smooth the surface with the blade of a knife. Bake in the oven for 55 minutes. When the cake comes out of the oven it will wobble slightly. Before turning it out, leave it to set in the fridge for at least 2 hours.

Chef's tip

Decorate with slices of fresh pineapple, grated coconut and a caramel coulis (see page 12).
For a coconut cake, make the recipe without the pineapple, reducing the cooking time by 5 minutes.

Magic Strawberry and Rhubarb Tart

Serves 8
Preparation: 40 minutes
Cooking time: 35 + 55 minutes

Rhubarb fondant
400 g (14 oz) rhubarb, peeled and
  cut into 3 cm (1¼ in) chunks
80 g (3 oz) brown sugar
30 ml (1 fl oz) water

Tart
250 g (9 oz) rich shortcrust pastry
1 vanilla pod
300 ml (10 fl oz) milk
3 eggs, separated
90 g (3¼ oz) caster (superfine)
  sugar
35 g (1¼ oz) honey
90 g (3¼ oz) butter
80 g (3 oz) plain (all-purpose)
  flour
pinch of salt
30 g (1 oz) ground almonds

Garnish
275 g (10 oz) Chantilly cream
  (see page 36)
200 g (7 oz) strawberries

11 cm (4 in) x 35 cm (14 in)
rectangular tart tin, greased with
butter

Put the rhubarb into a saucepan with the brown sugar and water and cook over a low heat until the water has entirely evaporated and the rhubarb is soft.

Preheat the oven to 180°C (350°F/Gas 4).

Line your baking tray with the pastry, cover with baking parchment and baking beans (to keep the pastry flat while blind baking) and put in the oven for 15 minutes.

Lower the oven temperature to 150°C (300°F/Gas 2).

Split the vanilla pod down the middle and scrape out the seeds with the blade of a knife. Heat the milk with the vanilla seeds and the pod. Bring to the boil, then immediately remove from the heat and leave to infuse. Set aside.

Beat the egg yolks with the sugar and honey until the mixture whitens. Melt the butter and pour it into the mixture. Then add the flour and salt. Beat for a few minutes more. Pour in the vanilla-infused milk little by little, having first removed the vanilla pod. The batter should be nice and smooth.

Beat the egg whites until stiff and, using a whisk, gently incorporate them into the batter. Sprinkle the ground almonds over the bottom of the greased tart tin. Then add the rhubarb fondant, and pour the batter on top. Smooth the surface with the blade of a knife and bake in the oven for 55 minutes. Allow to cool completely.

When the cake is cooled, pour the Chantilly cream (see page 36) over the tart and sprinkle with slices of strawberry. Serve chilled.

Pear and Speculoos Mini Cakes

Serves 8
Preparation: 30 minutes
Cooking time: 35 minutes
Resting time: 1 hour

Speculoos paste
200 g (7 oz) Speculoos or similar
   caramelised biscuits
150 ml (5 fl oz) unsweetened
   condensed milk
1 tablespoon honey
½ teaspoon ground cinnamon
pinch of salt

Mini Cakes
3 eggs, separated
75 g (2½ oz) caster (superfine)
   sugar
90 g (3¼ oz) butter
50 g (2 oz) plain (all-purpose)
   flour
pinch of salt
300 ml (10 fl oz) milk, at room
temperature
2 small pears, peeled, cored and
   diced

Mini cake tins, silicone or greased
with butter and lined with baking
parchment

Put the ingredients for the Speculoos paste in a blender and blitz to a smooth paste. Set aside.

Preheat the oven to 150°C (300°F/Gas 2).

For the cakes, beat the egg yolks with the sugar until the mixture whitens. Melt the butter and pour it into the mixture then add 150 g (5 oz) of the Speculoos paste. Then fold in the flour and salt. Beat together for a few minutes more. Pour the milk in little by little, whisking constantly.

Beat the egg whites until stiff and, using a whisk, gently incorporate them into the batter. Sprinkle the diced pear into the bottom of the buttered cake tins. Pour the batter on top, distributing equally between each tin. Smooth the surface with the blade of a knife. Bake in the oven for 35 minutes.

When you take them out of the oven, the cakes will wobble slightly. Before turning them out of the tin, put in the fridge for at least 1 hour, to set. Serve chilled.

Chef's tip

Spread the remaining Speculoos paste over the cakes.

You can also decorate them with crushed Speculoos biscuits and slices of pear.

Red Berry Cake

Serves 6
Preparation: 20 minutes
Cooking time: 30 minutes
Resting time: 1 hour

3 eggs, separated
95 g (3¼ oz) caster (superfine)
   sugar
90 g (3¼ oz) butter
95 g (3¼ oz) plain (all-purpose)
   flour
pinch of salt
180 g (6¼ oz) mixed berries
370 ml (12½ fl oz) milk, at room
   temperature

6 hemisphere tins in silicone,
greased with butter

Preheat the oven to 150°C (300°F/Gas 2).

Beat the egg yolks with the sugar until the mixture whitens. Melt the butter and pour it into the mixture. Then add the flour and salt. Beat for a few minutes more. Pour in the milk little by little, whisking constantly.

Beat the egg whites until stiff and, using a whisk, gently incorporate them into the batter. Sprinkle the red berries inside the greased tins. Pour the batter on top, then smooth the surface with the blade of a knife. The red berries will rise into the middle of the cakes during baking.

Bake in the oven for 30 minutes. Before turning them out of the tin, put in the fridge for at least 1 hour, to set. Serve chilled.

Chef's tip

Serve with a red berry coulis: place 200 g (7 oz) raspberries and 100 g (3½ oz) redcurrants in a saucepan with 100 g (3½ oz) caster (superfine) sugar. Set over a medium heat, stirring until the sugar has dissolved and the berries have become saucy. Taste and add more sugar if the berries are a little bit sharp. Strain the sauce through a sieve and chill until ready to serve.

Decorate the cakes with fresh red currants, raspberries and slices of strawberries.

Orange and Cinnamon Cake

Serves 8
Preparation: 25 minutes
Cooking time: 55 minutes
Resting time: 1 + 2 hours

1 orange
400 ml (13 fl oz) milk
2½ teaspoons ground cinnamon
4 eggs, separated
125 g (4 oz) caster (superfine)
   sugar
125 g (4 oz) butter
120 g (4 oz) plain (all-purpose)
   flour
pinch of salt

20 cm (8 in) square cake tin,
silicone or greased with butter and
lined with baking parchment

Wash the orange and cut off the zest in long strips. Heat the milk in a saucepan with the orange zest and cinnamon. Then leave off the heat to infuse for at least 1 hour.

Preheat the oven to 150°C (300°F/Gas 2).

Beat the egg yolks with the sugar until the mixture whitens. Melt the butter and pour it into the mixture. Then add the flour and salt. Beat for a few minutes more. Remove the zest from the milk then pour it in little by little, whisking constantly. Squeeze the orange then pour 100 ml (3½ fl oz) juice into the batter.

Beat the egg whites until stiff and, using a whisk, gently incorporate them into the batter. Pour the batter into the greased cake tin, smooth the surface with the blade of a knife and bake in the oven for 55 minutes. When the cake comes out of the oven it will wobble slightly.

Before turning it out, leave it to set in the fridge for at least 2 hours.

Chef's tip

Decorate the cake with slices of orange poached in sugar syrup. To make the sugar syrup, combine 250 ml (8½ fl oz/1 cup) water and 220 g (8 oz/1 cup) caster (superfine) sugar in a saucepan. Stir over a low heat until the sugar dissolves. Bring to the boil and cook for 2 minutes. Remove from the heat and cool until ready to use.

Apricot and Orange Blossom Cake

Serves 8
Preparation: 25 minutes
Cooking time: 55 minutes
Resting time: 2 hours

3 eggs, separated
95 g (3¼ oz) caster (superfine) sugar
1 tablespoon orange blossom water
95 g (3¼ oz) butter
90 g (3¼ oz) plain (all-purpose) flour
pinch of salt
370 ml (12½ fl oz) milk, at room temperature
410 g (14½ oz) can apricots in syrup

Savarin cake tin, 22 cm (8¾ in) diameter, silicone or greased with butter and lined with baking parchment

Preheat the oven to 150°C (300°F/Gas 2).

Beat the egg yolks with the sugar and orange water until the mixture whitens. Melt the butter and pour it into the mixture. Then add the flour and salt. Beat for a few minutes more. Pour in the milk little by little, whisking constantly.

Beat the egg whites until stiff and, using a whisk, gently incorporate them into the batter. Set aside a quarter of the apricots in syrup for decoration. Dice the remaining apricots, then sprinkle them over the bottom of the greased Savarin tin. Pour the batter on top, smooth the surface with the blade of a knife and bake in the oven for 55 minutes. When the cake comes out of the oven it will wobble slightly.

Before turning it out, leave it to set in the fridge for at least 2 hours.

Chef's tip

Serve with Chantilly cream: whip 284 ml (10 fl oz) whipping cream with the seeds scraped from 1 vanilla pod. Add icing (confectioners') sugar to taste.

Decorate with the remaining apricots and crushed pistachio nuts.

Raspberry and Matcha Tea Cake

Serves 10
Preparation: 25 minutes
Cooking time: 50 minutes
Resting time: 2 hours

4 eggs, separated
150 g (5 oz) caster (superfine)
    sugar
1 tablespoon water
125 g (4 oz) butter
100 g (3½ oz) plain (all-purpose)
    flour
pinch of salt
15 g (½ oz) matcha tea
500 ml (17 fl oz) milk, at room
    temperature
200 g (7 oz) fresh raspberries

11 cm (4 in) x 35 cm (14 in)
rectangular cake tin, silicone or
greased with butter or lined with
baking parchment

Preheat the oven to 150°C (300°F/Gas 2).

Whisk the egg yolks with the sugar and water until the mixture whitens. Melt the butter and pour it into the mixture. Then add the flour, salt and matcha tea. Beat for a few minutes more. Pour in the milk little by little, whisking constantly.

Beat the egg whites until stiff and, using a whisk, gently incorporate them into the batter.

Arrange the raspberries in the bottom of the greased cake tin and pour the batter on top. The raspberries will rise into the middle of the cake during baking. Smooth the surface of the batter with the blade of a knife and bake in the oven for 50 minutes. When the cake comes out of the oven it will wobble slightly.

Before turning it out, leave it to set in the fridge for at least 2 hours. Serve chilled.

Chef's tip

Decorate with a few raspberries and a red berry coulis (see page 32).

You could also make a white chocolate icing: melt 150 g (5 oz) white chocolate. Away from the heat, add 70 ml (2¼ fl oz) whipping cream. Chill in the fridge for at least 2 hours, then whip the ganache for around 10 minutes until it thickens.

Pistachio and Morello Cherry Cake

Serves 8
Preparation: 20 minutes
Cooking time: 55 minutes
Resting time: 2 hours

4 eggs, separated
135 g (4¾ oz) caster (superfine)
    sugar
125 g (4 oz) butter
1 heaped teaspoon pistachio
    paste (from a specialist grocer)
    or pistachio flavouring
40 g (1½ oz) ground pistachios
120 g (4 oz) plain (all-purpose)
    flour
pinch of salt
500 ml (17 fl oz) milk, at room
    temperature
200 g (7 oz) fresh morello
    cherries, stones removed
    (can also use tinned or jarrred
    cherries)

24 cm (9½ in) round cake tin,
silicone or greased with butter and
lined with baking parchment

Preheat the oven to 150°C (300°F/Gas 2).

Beat the egg yolks with the sugar until the mixture whitens. Melt the butter then pour it into the mixture. Add the pistachio paste followed by the ground pistachios, flour and salt. Beat for a few minutes more. Pour in the milk little by little, whisking constantly.

Beat the egg whites until stiff and, using a whisk, gently incorporate them into the batter.

Arrange the morello cherries at the bottom of the greased cake tin. Pour the batter on top, then smooth the surface with the blade of a knife. Bake in the oven for 55 minutes. When the cake comes out of the oven it will wobble slightly.

Before turning it out, leave it to set in the fridge for at least 2 hours.

Chef's tip

Decorate with Chantilly cream (see page 36), crushed pistachios and fresh cherries.

Magic Galette des Rois

Serves 8
Preparation: 30 minutes
Cooking time: 10 + 55 minutes
Resting time: 2 hours

Base
150 g (5 oz) petit beurre biscuits
   (French butter cookies)
30 g (1 oz) ground almonds
50 g (2 oz) salted butter, melted
2 pinches of fleur de sel

Topping
3 eggs, separated
110 g (3¾ oz) caster (superfine)
   sugar
90 g (3¼ oz) butter
1 teaspoon bitter almond extract
1 tablespoon rum (optional)
80 g (3 oz) plain (all-purpose)
   flour
pinch of salt
350 ml (11½ fl oz) almond milk

24 cm (9½ in) cake tin lined with
baking parchment

Preheat the oven to 150°C (300°F/Gas 2).

For the base, blitz all the ingredients together until smooth and pour in the crumbly mix into the lined caked tin. Press down on the mixture with the back of a tablespoon to spread it evenly over the bottom of the tin. Bake in the oven for 10 minutes.

For the topping, beat the egg yolks with the sugar until the mixture whitens. Melt the butter and pour it into the mixture followed by the almond extract and rum, if using. Then add the flour and salt. Beat for a few minutes more, then pour in the almond milk little by little, whisking constantly.

Beat the egg whites until stiff and, using a whisk, gently incorporate them into the batter. Pour the batter onto the biscuit base, then smooth the surface with the blade of a knife. Bake in the oven for 55 minutes. When the cake comes out of the oven it will wobble slightly. Before turning it out, leave it to set in the fridge for at least 2 hours. Serve chilled or gently reheated!

Chef's tip

Dust the cake with icing (confectioners') sugar and decorate with toasted almond flakes.

Magic Gingerbread Cake

Serves 10
Preparation: 20 minutes
Cooking time: 50 minutes
Resting time: 2 hours

3 eggs, separated
30 g (1 oz) caster (superfine) sugar
40 g (1½ oz) brown sugar
3 tablespoons honey
90 g (3¼ oz) butter
80 g (3 oz) plain (all-purpose) flour
pinch of salt
2 teaspoons French four-spice mix (pepper, cloves, nutmeg and ginger)
1 teaspoon ground cinnamon
350 ml (11½ fl oz) warm milk

20 cm (8 in) rectangle cake tin, silicone or greased with butter and lined with baking parchment

Preheat the oven to 150°C (300°F/Gas 2).

Beat the egg yolks with the sugar until the mixture whitens. Add the honey and beat some more. Melt the butter and pour it into the mixture. Then add the flour, salt, four-spice mix and cinnamon. Beat for a few more minutes. Pour in the milk little by little, whisking constantly.

Beat the egg whites until stiff and, using a whisk, gently incorporate them into the batter. Pour the batter into the greased cake tin and smooth the surface with the blade of a knife. Bake in the oven for 50 minutes. When the cake comes out of the oven it will wobble slightly.

Before turning it out, leave it to set in the fridge for at least 2 hours. Serve chilled.

Lemon Meringue Cake

Serves 10
Preparation: 40 minutes
Cooking time: 15 + 50 minutes
Resting time: 15 minutes

250 g (9 oz) rich shortcrust pastry
3 eggs, separated
70 g (2½ oz) caster (superfine)
   sugar
1 tablespoon water
70 g (2½ oz) butter
70 g (2½ oz) plain (all-purpose)
   flour
pinch of salt
275 ml (9 fl oz) milk, at room
   temperature
2 lemons

Meringue
2 egg whites
50 g (2 oz) caster (superfine) sugar
50 g (2 oz) icing (confectioners')
   sugar

27 cm (10½ in) round tart tin

Preheat the oven to 180°C (350°F/Gas 4).

Line the tart tin with the shortcrust pastry, cover with baking parchment and baking beans to keep the pastry flat while blind baking and bake in the oven for 15 minutes. Set aside in the fridge.

Lower the oven temperature to 150°C (300°F/Gas 2).

Whisk the egg yolks with the sugar and water until the mixture whitens. Melt the butter and pour it into the mixture. Add the flour and salt, then beat for a few minutes more. Pour in the milk little by little, whisking constantly. Add the zest of one of the lemons and the juice of both.

Beat the egg whites until stiff and, using a whisk, gently incorporate them into the batter.

Take the pastry out of the fridge and pour the batter in. Bake in the oven for 50 minutes. When it comes out of the oven, the cake may be slightly wobbly. Leave it to cool before putting the meringue on top.

For the meringue, beat the egg whites until stiff, gradually adding the two types of sugar until stiff peaks form when you take out the whisk. Spoon the meringue onto the top of the cake and brown with a kitchen blowtorch, or put the cake under the grill for 3–5 minutes.

Chef's tip

Decorate with the rind of the second lemon.

Intense Chocolate Easter Cake

Serves 8
Preparation: 25 minutes
Cooking time: 55 minutes
Resting time: 2 hours

4 eggs, separated
80 g (3 oz) caster (superfine) sugar
70 g (2½ oz) brown sugar
1 tablespoon water
125 g (4 oz) butter
70 g (2½ oz) plain (all-purpose) flour
pinch of salt
40 g (1½ oz) unsweetened cocoa powder
500 ml (17 fl oz) milk, at room temperature

20 cm (8 in) square cake tin, silicone or greased with butter and lined with baking parchment

Preheat the oven to 150°C (300°F/Gas 2).

Beat the egg yolks with the sugar and water until the mixture whitens. Melt the butter and pour it into the mixture. Then add the flour, cocoa and salt. Beat for a few minutes more. Pour in the milk little by little, whisking constantly.

Beat the egg whites until stiff and, using a whisk, gently incorporate them into the batter. Pour the batter into the cake tin and smooth the surface with the blade of a knife. Bake in the oven for 55 minutes. When the cake comes out of the oven it will wobble slightly.

Before turning it out, leave it to set in the fridge for at least 2 hours. Serve chilled.

Chef's tip

For the decoration, make some chocolate flakes with a vegetable peeler.

You can also make a whipped chocolate ganache by mixing 100 g (3½ oz) melted dark chocolate, 80 ml (2¾ fl oz) warmed whipping cream and 80 ml (2¾ fl oz) chilled cream. Set aside in the fridge for 2 hours then whip until it thickens.

Magic Cheesecake

Serves 8
Preparation: 40 minutes
Cooking time: 10 + 50 minutes
Resting time: 2 hours

Base
200 g (7 oz) Speculoos or similar
    caramelised biscuits
70 g (2½ oz) butter, melted

Topping
3 eggs, separated
100 g (3½ oz) caster (superfine)
    sugar
200 g (7 oz) full-fat cream cheese
70 g (2½ oz) plain (all-purpose
    flour
pinch of salt
250 ml (8½ fl oz) whole (full-fat)
    milk at, room temperature

24 cm (9½ in) cake tin greased
with butter and lined with baking
parchment

Preheat the oven to 150°C (300°F/Gas 2).

Blend the Speculoos biscuits with the melted butter to form a paste, then spread over the bottom of the lined tin. Pat the paste down well with the back of a tablespoon then bake in the oven for 10 minutes.

Beat the egg yolks with the sugar until the mixture whitens. Incorporate the cream cheese, flour and salt. Beat for a few minutes more. Pour in the milk little by little, whisking constantly.

Beat the egg whites until stiff and, using a whisk, gently incorporate them into the batter. Pour the lot into the tin on top of the Speculoos base. Bake in the oven for 50 minutes. When the cake comes out of the oven it will wobble slightly.

Leave it to set in the fridge for at least 2 hours. Serve chilled or gently warmed.

Chef's tip

Dust with icing (confectioners') sugar.

Magic Halloween Cake

Serves 8
Preparation: 40 minutes
Cooking time: 30 + 50 minutes
Resting time: 2 hours

300 g (10½ oz) pumpkin flesh,
   peeled and chopped into
   5cm (2 in) squares
1 vanilla pod
400 ml (13 fl oz) milk
4 eggs, separated
75 g (2½ oz) caster (superfine)
   sugar
50 g (2 oz) honey
125 g (4 oz) butter
115 g (4 oz) plain (all-purpose)
   flour
pinch of salt
2 teaspoons French four-spice mix
   (pepper, cloves, nutmeg and
   ginger)

24 cm (9½ in) cake tin, silicone or
greased with butter and lined with
baking parchment

Steam the pumpkin cubes for around 30 minutes. Purée with an electric hand blender.

Meanwhile, preheat the oven to 150°C (300°F/Gas 2).

Split the vanilla pod down the middle and scrape out the seeds with the blade of a knife. Heat the milk with the vanilla seeds and the pod. Bring to the boil, then immediately remove from the heat and leave to infuse.

Beat the egg yolks with the sugar until the mixture whitens. Then add the honey. Melt the butter and pour it into the mixture. Add the puréed pumpkin, flour, salt and four-spice. Remove the vanilla pod and pour in the milk little by little, whisking constantly.

Beat the egg whites until stiff and, using a whisk, gently incorporate them into the batter. Pour the batter into the cake tin and smooth the surface with the blade of a knife. Bake in the oven for 50 minutes. When the cake comes out of the oven it will wobble slightly.

Before turning it out, leave it to set in the fridge for at least 2 hours. Serve chilled.

Chef's tip

For a cream cheese icing, whip 80 ml (2¾ fl oz) chilled whipping cream until it thickens. Add 150 g (5 oz) cream cheese, then 20 g (¾ oz) icing (confectioners') sugar, whipping constantly. You can also decorate the cake with pumpkin jam.

Magic Cannelés

Serves 8
Preparation: 25 minutes
Cooking time: 23 minutes
Resting time: 1 + 1 hour

1 vanilla pod
180 ml (6 fl oz) whole (full-fat
  milk
1 teaspoon vanilla extract
20 ml (¾ fl oz) rum
45 g (1¾ oz) butter
2 eggs, separated
50 g (2 oz) caster (superfine) sugar
60 g (2 oz) plain (all-purpose)
  flour
pinch of salt
brown sugar, for the moulds

Silicone cannelé moulds, greased
with butter

Split the vanilla pod down the middle and scrape out the seeds with the blade of a knife. Heat the milk in a saucepan with the vanilla seeds, pod, vanilla extract and rum. Then leave off the heat to infuse for at least 1 hour.

Preheat the oven to 150°C (300°F/Gas 2).

Heat the butter in a saucepan until it starts to turn a nice hazelnut colour. Leave to cool. Beat the egg yolks with the sugar until the mixture whitens, then pour in the melted butter. Add the flour and salt. Beat for a few minutes more. Remove the vanilla pod then pour in the milk little by little, whisking constantly.

Beat the egg whites until stiff and, using a whisk, gently incorporate them into the batter. Sprinkle the cannelé moulds with brown sugar. Fill each mould three-quarters the way to the top with the batter. Smooth the surface of each cannelé with the back of a teaspoon. Bake in the oven for 23 minutes.

Before turning them out, leave to set in the fridge for at least 1 hour.

Chef's tip

Serve the cannelés with a caramel coulis (see page 12) and sprinkle with cinnamon.

Magic Log Cake

Preparation: 35 minutes
Cooking time: 50 minutes
Resting time: 2 hours

1 vanilla pod
350 ml (11½ fl oz) milk
3 eggs, separated
1 teaspoon water
45 g (1¾ oz) caster (superfine)
   sugar
100 g (3½ oz) sweetened chestnut
   purée
90 g (3¼ oz) butter
70 g (2½ oz) plain (all-purpose)
   flour
pinch of salt
60 g (2 oz) marrons glacés, broken
   into small pieces

Yule log cake tin, silicone or
greased with butter and lined with
baking parchment

Preheat the oven to 160°C (320°F/Gas 3).

Split the vanilla pod down the middle and scrape out the seeds with
the blade of a knife. Heat the milk with the vanilla seeds and the pod.
Bring to the boil, then immediately remove from the heat and leave
to infuse.

Whisk the egg yolks with the sugar and water until the mixture
whitens. Then add the chestnut purée. Melt the butter and pour it
into the mixture. Add the flour and salt then beat for a few minutes.
Remove the vanilla pod then pour in the milk little by little, whisking
constantly. Beat the egg whites until stiff and, using a whisk, gently
incorporate them into the batter.

Sprinkle the bottom of the Yule log tin with broken marrons glacés,
then pour in the batter. Smooth the surface with the blade of a knife.
Bake in the oven for 50 minutes. When the cake comes out of the oven
it will wobble slightly.

Before turning it out, leave it to set in the fridge for at least 2 hours.
Serve chilled.

Chef's tip

You can also make an icing by whipping 200 ml (7 fl oz) whipping cream
with 120 g (4 oz) mascarpone until the mixture thickens, then gradually
adding 30 g (1 oz) caster (superfine) sugar, whipping constantly.

Decorate with a few whole marrons glacés or broken pieces.

Magic Brownies

Serves 10
Preparation: 25 minutes
Cooking time: 10 + 55 minutes
Resting time: 2 hours

80 g (3 oz) walnuts, crushed
4 eggs, separated
125 g (4 oz) caster (superfine)
  sugar
1 tablespoon water
125 g (4 oz) butter
110 g (3¾ oz) plain (all-purpose)
  flour
30 g (1 oz) unsweetened cocoa
  powder
pinch of salt
500 ml (17 fl oz) milk, at room
  temperature
50 g (2 oz) chocolate chips

20 cm (8 in) square cake tin
silicone or greased with butter and
lined with baking parchment

Preheat the oven to 150°C (300°F/Gas 2).

Toast the walnuts in the oven, on a baking tray, for about 10 minutes. Beat the egg yolks with the sugar and water until the mixture whitens. Melt the butter and pour it into the mixture. Add the flour, cocoa and salt. Beat for a few minutes more. Pour in the milk little by little, whisking constantly.

Beat the egg whites until stiff and, using a whisk, gently incorporate them into the batter. Arrange the crushed walnuts and chocolate chips in the bottom of the tin. Cover with the batter and smooth the surface with the blade of a knife. Bake in the oven for 55 minutes. When the cake comes out of the oven it will wobble slightly.

Before turning it out, leave it to set in the fridge for at least 2 hours. Turn out the cake then cut into small squares.

Chef's tip

Serve with Chantilly cream (see page 32), melted chocolate and a few crushed walnuts.

Magic Red Velvet Cake

Serves 8
Preparation: 40 minutes
Cooking time: 50 minutes
Resting time: 1 + 2 hours

1 vanilla pod
500 ml (17 fl oz) milk
4 eggs, separated
150 g (5 oz) caster (superfine)
 sugar
1 tablespoon liquid red food
 colouring
125 g (4 oz) butter
115 g (4 oz) plain (all-purpose)
 flour
10 g (½ oz) unsweetened cocoa
 powder
pinch of salt
a drop of powdered red food
 colouring

Icing
300 ml (10 fl oz) whipping cream
150 g (5 oz) mascarpone
45 g (1¾ oz) caster (superfine)
 sugar

2 x 17 cm (6¾ in) cake tins,
silicone or greased with butter and
lined with baking parchment

Split the vanilla pod down the middle and scrape out the seeds with the blade of a knife. Heat the milk with the vanilla seeds and the pod. Bring to the boil, then immediately remove from the heat and leave to infuse for at least 1 hour.

Preheat the oven to 150°C (300°F/Gas 2).

Beat the egg yolks with the sugar and liquid food colouring until the mixture whitens. Melt the butter and pour it into the mixture. Add the flour, cocoa and salt. Beat for a few minutes more. Remove the vanilla pod then pour in the milk little by little, whisking constantly.

Beat the egg whites until stiff with the powdered food colouring. Using a whisk, incorporate them gently into the batter. Pour the batter evenly into the cake tins and smooth the surface with the blade of a knife. Bake in the oven for 50 minutes. When they come out of the oven, the cakes will wobble slightly.

Before turning them out, put them in the fridge for at least 2 hours to set.

In the meantime, prepare the icing. Whip the cream until it thickens. Add the mascarpone, whipping constantly. Finally pour in the sugar, and whip for a further 30 seconds. Spread half of the icing on the first cake. Place the second cake on top and cover with the rest of the icing. Serve chilled.

Chef's tip

Decorate with red coloured sugar and a mixture of red berries.

Marshmallow Cake

Serves 8
Preparation: 25 minutes
Cooking time: 5 + 45 minutes
Resting time: 2 hours

500 ml (17 fl oz) milk
150 g (5 oz) marshmallows
4 eggs, separated
40 g (1½ oz) caster (superfine)
   sugar
1 tablespoon water
125 g (4 oz) butter
80 g (3 oz) plain (all-purpose)
   flour
pinch of salt

24 cm (9½ in) cake tin, silicone or
greased with butter and lined with
baking parchment

Preheat the oven to 150°C (300°F/Gas 2).

Simmer the marshmallows in milk in a saucepan until totally melted. Leave to cool.

Meanwhile, beat the egg yolks with the sugar and water until the mixture whitens. Melt the butter and pour it into the mixture. Then add the flour and salt. Beat for a few minutes more. Pour in the milk and marshmallow mixture little by little, whisking constantly.

Beat the egg whites until stiff and, using a whisk, gently incorporate them into the batter. Pour into the buttered cake tin, smooth the surface with the blade of a knife and bake in the oven for 45 minutes. When the cake comes out of the oven it will wobble slightly.

Before turning it out, leave it to set in the fridge for at least 2 hours.

Chef's tip

Dust with icing (confectioners') sugar.

You can also decorate with a few marshmallows lightly browned with a kitchen blowtorch or from under a grill.

Mango and Passion Fruit Heart Cake

Serves 8
Preparation: 30 minutes
Cooking time: 50 minutes
Resting time: 2 hours

3 eggs, separated
75 g (2½ oz) caster (superfine)
   sugar
90 g (3¼ oz) butter
95 g (3¼ oz) plain (all-purpose)
   flour
pinch of salt
320 ml (11 fl oz) milk, at room
   temperature
180 g (6¼ oz) passion fruits
1 ripe mango, peeled

24 cm (9½ in) heart-shaped cake
tin, silicone or greased with butter
and lined with baking parchment

Preheat the oven to 150°C (300°F/Gas 2).

Beat the egg yolks with the sugar until the mixture whitens. Melt the butter and pour it into the mixture. Then add the flour and salt. Beat for a few minutes more. Pour in the milk little by little, whisking constantly.

Cut the passion fruits in half and scoop them into a fine sieve over a bowl. Press the fruit against the sides of the sieve with a flexible spatula to extract the juice. You should be able to extract 40 ml (1¼ fl oz) of liquid. Pour this juice into the batter.

Beat the egg whites until stiff and, using a whisk, gently incorporate them into the batter.

Set aside a quarter of the mango for decoration and cut the rest of the flesh into small dice. Scatter the pieces into the cake tin. Pour the batter on top, then smooth the surface with the blade of a knife. Bake in the oven for 50 minutes. When the cake comes out of the oven it will wobble slightly.

Before turning it out, leave it to set in the fridge for at least 2 hours. Serve chilled.

Chef's tip

Decorate with passion fruit and strips of mango. You can also make a topping by melting 100 g (3½ oz) white chocolate in 50 ml (2 fl oz) whipping cream in a bain-marie with a little orange food colouring.

Olives, Lardons and Feta

Serves 10
Preparation: 25 minutes
Cooking time: 50 minutes
Resting time: 2 hours

3 eggs, separated
1 tablespoon olive oil
100 g (3½ oz) salted butter,
  melted
90 g (3¼ oz) plain (all-purpose)
  flour
1 tablespoon snipped basil
sea salt and freshly ground black
  pepper
350 ml (11½ fl oz) milk, at room
  temperature
125 g (4 oz) green olives
125 g (4 oz) lardons (matchsticks
  of pork belly)
125 g (4 oz) feta, diced

20 cm (8 in) rectangle cake tin,
silicone or greased with butter and
lined with baking parchment

Preheat the oven to 150°C (300°F/Gas 2).

Beat the egg yolks with the olive oil and melted butter until the mixture is smooth. Add the flour and basil and season generously with salt and pepper. Beat for a few minutes more. Gradually pour in the milk, whisking constantly.

Beat the egg whites until stiff and, using a whisk, gently incorporate them into the batter.

Cut the olives in half. Put them in the bottom of the cake tin. Lightly brown the lardons in a frying pan then sprinkle them over the olives. Add the diced feta. Pour the batter over the olives, lardons and feta, then smooth the surface with the blade of a knife. Bake in the oven for 50 minutes. When the tart comes out of the oven it will wobble slightly.

Before turning it out, leave it to set in the fridge for at least 2 hours. Serve chilled.

Chef's tip

Serve this cake with a cucumber, spring onion and feta salad accompaniment. Garnish with a few fennel fronds and drizzle with olive oil.

Goats' Cheese and Figs

Serves 10
Preparation: 25 minutes
Cooking time: 50 minutes
Resting time: 2 hours

3 eggs, separated
3 level tablespoons honey
70 g (2½ oz) butter, melted
120 g (4 oz) fresh goats' cheese
50 g (2 oz) plain (all-purpose)
  flour
2 pinches of *herbes de Provence*
  (French herb mix)
370 ml (12½ fl oz) milk, at room
  temperature
100 g (3½ oz) dried figs, cut into
  small pieces
75 g (2½ oz) goats' cheese log,
  diced
sea salt and freshly ground black
  pepper

22 cm (10 in) Savarin tin, silicone
or greased with butter and lined
with baking parchment

Preheat the oven to 150°C (300°F/Gas 2).

Beat the egg yolks with the honey and melted butter until the mixture is smooth. Incorporate the goats' cheese. Add the flour, then the salt, pepper and *herbes de Provence*. Beat for a few more minutes. Gradually pour in the milk, whisking constantly.

Beat the egg whites until stiff and, using a whisk, gently incorporate them into the batter.

Scatter the pices of fig in the bottom of the cake tin followed by the diced goats' cheese. Pour the batter on top. Bake in the oven for 50 minutes. When the tart comes out of the oven it will wobble slightly.

Before turning it out, leave it to set in the fridge for at least 2 hours. Serve chilled.

Chef's tip

If you prefer, replace half of the goats' cheese with Roquefort.

Serve with a red leaf salad, some dried figs and feta.

Garnish with fresh parseley.

Magic Mustard Quiche

Serves 10
Preparation: 25 minutes
Cooking time: 20 + 55 minutes

250 g (9 oz) puff pastry
3 eggs, separated
1 tablespoon olive oil
85 g (3 oz) salted butter, melted
80 g (3 oz) mustard
70 g (2½ oz) plain (all-purpose)
    flour
300 ml (10 fl oz) milk at room
    temperature
100 g (3½ oz) ham, diced
130 g (4¼ oz) Gruyère, grated
10 sun-dried tomatoes, cut into
    small pieces
sea salt and freshly ground black
    pepper

27 cm (10½ in) tart tin

Preheat the oven to 180°C (350°F/Gas 4).

Line the tart tin with the pastry. Cover with baking parchment and baking beans to keep the pastry flat while blind baking, then bake in the oven for 20 minutes.

Lower the oven temperature to 150°C (300°F/Gas 2).

Separate the eggs. Beat the egg yolks with the olive oil and melted butter until the mixture is smooth. Then add the mustard, flour, salt and pepper. Beat for a few minutes more. Gradually pour in the milk, whisking constantly. Add the ham and 50 g (2 oz) of grated Gruyère cheese. Beat the egg whites until stiff and, using a whisk, gently incorporate them into the batter.

Spread the sun-dried tomatoes across the bottom of the tart tin. Pour the batter over them, then sprinkle the rest of the grated cheese on top. Bake in the oven for 55 minutes.

Leave to cool for a few moments before eating.

Chef's tip

Decorate the slices with grated cheese and serve with a rocket, mange tout and pumpkin seed salad. Drizzle over some olive oil.

Acknowledgements

Thanks to my parents, Loïc, Hubert, Fabien, Amélie, Jules, Laëtitia, Alban, Apolline and Jérémie for being my tasting team.

To Rita and her children, Christine, Maëlys, Annélia, Elodie, Fabienne, Virginie, Catherine, Claire and Laurent for trying out the recipes and giving me such good advice!

To the whole Marabout team for trusting in me and making this dream come true.

To Marlène and Valéry for making this book look so good.

To Guillaume, taster, multi-tester, adviser, chauffeur and commis chef! Thank you for your invaluable help.

And special thanks to my daughters Cloélia, Eléa and Callista for having eaten more magic cakes during the gestation of this book than anyone else will ever eat in a lifetime!

First published in 2013 by Hachette Books (Marabout)
This English language edition published in 2015 by Hardie Grant Books

Hardie Grant Books (UK)
5th & 6th Floors
52–54 Southwark Street
London SE1 1UN
www.hardiegrant.co.uk

Hardie Grant Books (Australia)
Ground Floor, Building 1
658 Church Street
Melbourne, VIC 3121
www.hardiegrant.com.au

The moral rights of Christelle Huet-Gomez to be identified as the author
of this work have been asserted by her in accordance with the
Copyright, Designs and Patents Act 1988.

British Library Cataloguing-in-Publication Data. A catalogue record
for this book is available from the British Library.

ISBN: 978-1-78488-017-0

Publisher: Kate Pollard
Senior Editor: Kajal Mistry
Translator: Gilla Evans
Typesetter: David Meikle
Copy Editor: Zelda Turner
Graphic design: WEAREMB
Illustrations: Léa Maupetit

Printed and bound in China by 1010

10 9 8 7 6 5 4 3 2